Tips From a Top Tycoon

Alexander Prosser's amanuenses are Simon Rose and Gail Renard. Simon Rose is a mercenary, specializing in journalism and is the author of the comic novel *Filthy Lucre*. Gail Renard is a TV comedy writer and performer and is a leading light in C.A.B., the Campaign for Alphabetical Billing. Seasoned and well-respected writers, they are well aware of Alexander Prosser's political incorrectness, but know that the reader will understand that his intention is only to teach, entertain, inform . . . and offend. The two are united in their grief at the passing of one of Britain's greatest entrepreneurs, and are currently contesting his will.

TIPS FROM A TOP TYCOON

How to be a Bastard in Business

ALEXANDER PROSSER

as told to Simon Rose and Gail Renard

Illustrations by Noel Ford

Grafton

An Imprint of HarperCollins*Publishers*

**Dedicated to Robert Maxwell
Who Showed the Way**

Grafton
An Imprint of HarperCollins*Publishers*,
77–85 Fulham Palace Road
Hammersmith, London W6 8JB

A Grafton Original 1992
9 8 7 6 5 4 3 2 1

A catalogue record for this book is
available from the British Library

ISBN 0 00 637810 2

Set in Century Old Style by
Rowland Phototypesetting Ltd
Bury St Edmunds, Suffolk

Printed in Great Britain by
HarperCollinsManufacturing Glasgow

Contents

Part One

IN THE BEGINNING

An Introduction

by Alexander Charles Prosser,

Chairman and Chief Executive, British Industrial Group

Throughout my glorious career, many people have come up to me and asked: 'I think you're wonderful, Mr Prosser. I'd love to be a top tycoon like you. How do I go about it?'

Up till now, my answer has always been the same: 'Not by giving away free advice to little turds like you for a start.'

But now I realize that that selfish attitude towards my fellow man was wrong and I have decided that I should share my business secrets. In making this momentous decision, I have been persuaded not only by my public spiritedness and my altruistic desire to help British businesses survive the recession, but also by an extremely healthy cheque from the publishers.

Now that I know it hasn't bounced, I am poised over my personal assistant, who is ready to take everything down. I will reveal all – to her and to you.

I intend to take you, step by step, through the various stages of becoming a tycoon. I shall tell you whether you have what it takes and show you how to go about achieving your life's dream.

There's almost no bit of business I haven't experienced: brewing, hotels, supermarkets, drugs, tobacco, old people's homes, private hospitals, nuclear waste management; whatever the flavour of the pie, if it looks tasty enough I'm likely to have my finger well and truly stuck into it.

It was Edward Heath who gave me the greatest compliment of my career when he referred to me as 'the unacceptable two faces of capitalism'.

I am not saying that I can turn you into Alexander Prosser – that

would be too much for anyone to hope for. But in my no-punches-pulled style, I will expound my well-tested theories of how to bribe, bully and browbeat your way up the ladder of business success.

IT WORKED FOR ME. IT CAN EVEN WORK FOR SOMEONE LIKE YOU.

GET CLIMBING!

1
Climbing the Ladder

Looking for Mr Right plc

What sort of virgin are you? Wise or foolish? The foolish virgin searching for her one true love leaps into bed with the first Mr Right who offers her any old position. The wise virgin, on the other hand, realizing she'll be stuck with Mr Right for the rest of her life, sensibly tries out a few interesting positions before coyly surrendering her maidenhood to her one and only true love.

As a novice taking your first step onto the corporate ladder, if you say 'yes' to the wrong Mr Right, you could end up wasting the best years of your life pushing paper in a company that's going nowhere fast.

Get it right and, in my capable hands, you could soon be on your way to fame, fortune and fun galore!

To have any hope of making it to the top of the greasy pole, you must check out the field thoroughly. Here are the all-important questions you, the budding tycoon, must ask before yielding your virginity to Mr Right plc.

Having found the position that you know will satisfy you, you can make your bed and lie back happily in it, giving your all, and dreaming of the day when you'll be the one on top.

THE ALL-IMPORTANT QUESTIONS THE CORPORATE VIRGIN NEEDS ANSWERED

Is it on a bus route?
Do they give luncheon vouchers?

Will you have your own office?
Will you have your own secretary?
Will you have your own way with your own secretary?
Does the Chairman take an active interest in promoting junior staff?
Has the Chairman ever been inside the offices of the junior staff?
Has the Chairman ever been inside?
How old is the Chairman?
How dicky is his heart?
Does he scare easily?
Does the Chairman's secretary talk in her sleep?
How big is the Chairman's family?
How big is his daughter?
Could you face sleeping with his daughter to find out what is going on?
Could you face sleeping with his son to find out what is going on?
Does the Chairman have a company helicopter?
Does the Chairman have a clue?
Do they promote to board level internally?
How many levels of promotion are there until you reach the board?
Does the firm send its executives on survival courses?
Does anyone ever fail to survive the survival courses?
What's the youngest member of the board they've ever had?
How many floors up is the management floor?
Do the windows on the management floor open?
Do they open wide enough to get a large object through?
What's on the menu in the executive dining room today?

HAVE YOU GOT WHAT IT TAKES?

Now that you've assessed the company you're joining, you're going to have to assess yourself.

In the old days, the tycoon-to-be could content himself with standing in front of the mirror each morning chanting 'Mirror, mirror on the wall, who's the biggest bastard of them all?' and then smashing it into smithereens when it doesn't give the right answer.

In today's tougher, more demanding, environment we need to util-

CHAIRMAN
CHAIRMAN
RIGHT
PLC

ize sharper, more modern, scientific techniques to assure ourselves that we've got what it takes.

I've got it – in spades. But have you? At considerable expense, I have had a rigorous self-assessment test prepared exclusively for this book by a team of eminent psychologists from Cambridge University.

Read each statement and mark it with a 'T' for true or 'F' for false, giving your instant reaction. Be completely honest with yourself, so that the quiz will be of real use. Complete the test in one sitting, free from distractions, allowing five minutes.

You have to be ruthless to be a tycoon. Be ruthless with yourself in this test, answer every statement honestly and it will reveal your hidden psychological profile and tell you whether or not you are fit to join me at the top.

WHICH OF THESE APPLY TO YOU?

Self-Assessment Test – Part One

- I fart when under stress
- I dream about the Royal Family
- I think of a glass of water as being half empty rather than half full
- I never think of a glass of water if I can help it
- I wouldn't tell the truth if my mother's life depended on it
- I miss my mother
- I am constantly preoccupied with thoughts of sex
- I am constantly preoccupied with thoughts of sex
- I am constantly preoccupied with thoughts of sex
- I feel ill if I don't have sex at least once an hour
- I feel ill
- I feel better now
- When bested in a business deal I tend to cry
- I cannot work with women whose shoulders are broader than mine
- I suffer form dyslecksia
- I have a bad memory
- I have a good memory
- I've remembered I'm a Womble

PORTRAIT OF A FAMILY

Your First Problem

Before you start clawing your way to the top, your loves, labours and loyalties are with your family. But from this moment on, the company is your family. And woe betide the employee whose real family doesn't come up to scratch.

Upon arrival at a new firm, the first thing many people do is plonk a photograph of their family down on their desk. Much as you love your family, your instincts should now be telling you that something is wrong.

Just looking at that picture staring at you all day, you should realize that your family, when photographed, may not come up to your exacting new standards, particularly if you accumulated them before you reached your present exalted position. If the best-looking person in your family photo is your dog, then you have a problem.

Nothing hurts a chap's progress more than the Chairman wincing when he picks up the picture frame on your desk. So how do you cope when it comes to having that all-important family portrait for your office if you have a family as ugly as sin – but not half as exciting?

Solution

Most model agencies are now well-used to requests from desperate up-and-coming executives wanting to purchase ready-made pictures of the ideal corporate family. For a modest fee, you can acquire a comely wife and a batch of happy, smiling children, all looking adoringly at their father. Depending on the image you want to project, you can choose the requisite setting from among such popular favourites as the garden of your country home, lolling around the Christmas tree or posing at the entrance to Disneyland (with Mickey and Goofy).

If your time is too precious to pose yourself, you don't even have to be present. Your face can be superimposed onto a suitable model's head for a small extra charge. It is important, however, to check the family photos of the other executives in your company, to make sure you are not about to buy the same family as a chap in the room next door.

You might become concerned about the approach of office parties and outings and the firm's annual dinner-dance. Do not panic at the thought of having to produce your ever-so photogenic family. Although it doesn't come cheap, the same models are available for various functions.

Note, too, a service which has proved popular with executives for many years, that of having photos of themselves taken with the rich and famous. (But do not make the same careless mistake as one young executive who, although only twenty-four years old, had a picture on his office wall of himself shaking hands with Winston Churchill.)

SPIKING YOUR RIVAL'S GUNS

Do you think it important to be nice to people on the way up in case you meet them again on the way down?

You do? Heaven help you.

That is the sort of stupid, wimpy, namby-pamby, attitude that will keep you sitting behind that cheap laminated teak desk of yours for the rest of what you laughingly call your career. What happened to those toughening-up exercises you are supposed to be doing?

You are not in business to make friends. From now on, you must understand that your colleagues are your deadliest enemies. They stand between you and your success. They must be eliminated, or nobbled at the very least.

No opportunity should be wasted to make your colleagues look ridiculous, moronic or even downright crooked, while you remain the blue-eyed boy. This requires thought, effort and skill. One slip and the knife could be in your back while your rival is welcomed on to the board.

Just as the army practises war games, so the budding executive should practise his shafting technique. Remember we're not talking paint guns here, we're talking Magnum 45s. Here's some target practice for you to improve your aim.

Your Mission

Tom, Dick and Harry are your closest colleagues and your best friends. The four of you share an office on the third floor next to the typing pool. It's a happy office, with plenty of bonhomie and repartee.

Until, that is, you hear that the four of you are being considered for promotion to the next rung up the corporate ladder. It will mean a bigger office, a bigger salary and a smaller secretary. It's what you've always wanted. The whiff of success is suddenly in your nostrils. You can almost smell the boardroom now.

But only one of you is going to be awarded the key to the executive lavatory. Is it going to be Tom, Dick, Harry or *you*?

Suddenly the laughter has gone out of the air.

Everyone is on tenterhooks, waiting for details of the promotion procedure to arrive. You waylay the office messenger in the mailroom and, distracting him, remove from his trolley a memo addressed to the four of you. On your way back to the office, you stop the lift between floors. Tearing it open with trembling hands, you read that a date and time has been set for the promotion board. Do you:

a) Show the others the memo, shake hands and say: 'I hope the best man wins'?
b) Eat the note?
c) Tell the bastards that the board is two days after it really is?

You could cut the atmosphere in the office with a knife. Although you are all trying to pretend that nothing has changed between you, everyone is dizzy from the effort of putting up a front, looking over their shoulders and watching their backs.

Your nerves are stretched to breaking point when Tom opens his briefcase and, with a flourish, suddenly whips out a vicious-looking knife.

Flinging yourself behind the nearest secretary, you feel foolish when he then produces a large cream cake with a candle on it and reminds you that it is your birthday. Do you:

a) Thank him profusely and insist on sharing it with Tom, Dick and Harry?

b) Give it to the Chairman's secretary to ingratiate yourself?
c) Wait until no one's looking, shove your fingers down your throat to make yourself violently sick and claim Tom has tried to poison you?

Your ploy works. Everyone in the office turns against Tom and sends him to Coventry.

He doesn't know what has hit him. In a desperate attempt to regain favour the crest-fallen Tom, full of false protestations of remorse, takes you to the lavatory to help you tidy up. Do you:

a) Say you hope to be able to do the same for him some time?
b) Shove your fingers down your throat *again* so that you are violently sick all over him?
c) Pull out your shirt tail and run from the lavatory screaming that he has made advances towards you?

You arrive at the office the next day to discover that Tom's desk has been cleared overnight. A new memo makes it clear that now only Dick, Harry and you are being considered for the post. The three of you decide to celebrate with a cup of Bovril.

As you are all standing at the vending machine, Dick claims to have left his wallet at home and asks to borrow money from you. You notice, out of the corner of your eye, the Chairman approaching. Do you:

a) Say pompously: 'Never a borrower nor a lender be'?
b) Say laughingly: 'Tell us that brilliant joke of yours about the Chairman and the plunger again!'?
c) Say, in a loud booming voice: 'If you still haven't got your drug addiction under control, I'm certainly not going to finance it'?

The Chairman blithely passes by with a cheery 'hello boys'. You kick yourself for forgetting just how deaf the old buffer has become.

Even though you are still convinced that you are the ideal candidate for the post, you are worried that the board might be taken in by the smooth, sophisticated veneer oozed by Dick and Harry.

Fortunately, glancing at the calendar, you notice the date is Febru-

ary 13th. You dash out to make a few purchases before the last post goes. Do you:

a) Send a Valentine from Dick to Tracey, the very plain personnel manageress, proposing marriage?
b) Send a Valentine from Dick to the entire typing pool, each proposing marriage?
c) Send a Valentine from Dick to all the male executives in the company, proposing marriage?

For the first time in a month, you turn up early for work to ensure that you can get a good ringside seat. You are not disappointed, although the fun ends more quickly than you might have hoped.

As Dick is carried away on a stretcher, you and Harry eye each other warily. You know it's going to be a fight to the finish.

Returning from lunch, you find that the office is in turmoil. There's a terrible fuss because the Chairman's wallet has apparently been stolen. You become a little concerned when you spot the Chairman and two security men coming towards you. In rushing to open the door for them, Harry bumps into you and, as he moves away you discover, to your alarm, the missing wallet in your pocket. Do you:

a) Panic and desperately try to swallow it?
b) Bump into the Chairman and slip the wallet back into his pocket?
c) Quickly whip a hundred pounds out and bump back into Harry just as the door opens?

The following day, a memo from the personnel department appears on the office notice board announcing that Harry has taken early retirement – aged twenty-six.

You go to the interview with the Chairman and personnel director with a song in your heart and a smile on your lips. But, to your chagrin, you are told that it is by no means certain that the post will be yours. If you don't come up to scratch at the interview, the post will be advertised outside.

Terrified that the prized post could slip from your grasp at the final hurdle, do you:

a) Stammer, babble and drool uncontrollably?
b) Cry?
c) Take out your handkerchief to stem the flow of tears, thus exposing to the Chairman's gaze the photograph which you found in his wallet, showing himself and a troop of extremely eager Boy Scouts?

To your delight and surprise, the Chairman shakes you by the hand and offers you the post on the spot, at double the anticipated salary. You deign to think about it, promising you'll get back to him in a day or so's time.

Game, set and match.

How did you do? Add up your score – one point for every (a), two for (b), three for (c).

7–12:	Please! Don't waste my time.
13–18:	Re-read the book up to this point, or if that's too difficult, get somebody to read it to you.
19–21:	That's my boy! However, how many times do I have to tell you that, as my son, you don't have to take these tests.
22 or over:	Either you can't count or you're cheating. It doesn't matter. Both are assets for running successful companies.

RAT OVERBOARD

– How To Tell If Your Company's Going Under

WARNING! No matter how brilliant an executive you are (and after reading and learning from this book you will be), if you're still climbing the ladder there's always the possibility some superannuated bozo higher up can screw up and scupper the company before you make it to the top seat, pulling you under with it.

Like any good rat, you want to be the first to abandon the sinking ship. So it's imperative that you learn how to recognize the danger signs and find yourself another vessel for your ambitions while your head's still above water.

JUST REMIND ME — WHICH FAT TUB OF LARD WITH A BRAIN THE SIZE OF A GNAT'S BELLY-BUTTON DID YOU SAY CAN'T RUN THIS COMPANY TO SAVE HIS BOOZE-SODDEN LIFE?
FRESH TEA

You know it's time to push the women and children out of the way and dash for the lifeboats when:

- You spot the Chairman bringing in sandwiches from home
- You see a photograph in the papers of the Chairman alighting from the new company helicopter
- You see a photograph in the papers of the Chairman alighting from a van with a blanket over his head
- You are ordered to use mini-cabs instead of taxis to save on expenses
- The first mini-cab you ride in is driven by the moonlighting Chief Executive
- The Annual Report arrives 'Postage Due'
- You spy the Finance Director playing Double or Quits with his secretary for her pay cheque
- The rubber plant is repossessed in the middle of a board meeting
- In the interests of economy, staff are asked to use both sides of scrap paper
- In the interests of economy, staff are asked to use both sides of the lavatory paper
- The factory is torched for the insurance money
- The factory is torched but the insurance premiums haven't been paid
- The Finance Director absconds with the company funds to the Cayman Islands
- The Finance Director absconds with the company funds to the Isle of Wight
- The company mascot is dish of the day in the canteen – for a week

2
Running the Office

Take Something Down Miss Jones

If you've made it this far without dropping by the wayside then you should by now appreciate the importance of having a good secretary under you.

By this stage, you should be able to pick your own secretary, rather than have one assigned to you by that woman running the typing pool whose finger you slammed in the filing cabinet when she tried to kiss you under the mistletoe at the last Christmas party.

The chances are that they'll want to be called your personal assistant. Fine. They should be encouraged to assist you extremely personally whenever the mood takes you. However, everyone knows that PA is a totally spurious title thought up by people wanting to prove their self-importance – much like the title of 'manager' which you covet so much.

A tottie to keep your lap warm is the first perk you've earned and you should enjoy it to the full. Hire 'em. Desire 'em. Fire 'em.

HOW TO CHOOSE A SECRETARY

Somewhere out there is the perfect secretary for you. But how do you find Miss Perfect? And how do you pin her down when you've found her?

It always amazes me how poor many businessmen are at choosing secretarial talent. How do you measure up? These two sample letters are taken from the exhaustive tests I dictated personally to every one of the hundreds of women who clamoured for the last vacant sec-

retarial post in my office. One of them was successful. Can you tell which one?

TEST 137: ENID

The Director
Dr Barnardo's
Tanner's Lane
Ilford

Dear Sir,

Amongst my mail this morning was your letter soliciting money to assist the poor and needy children in your care. I'm shocked to the quick. How dare you try to get money from me under false pretences? It is well known that the more disadvantaged the person is at the start of his life, the harder he strives to overcome his unfortunate start and the further he will go.

I feel, therefore, that on this occasion I must rein in my naturally generous spirit. A monetary contribution would undoubtedly be detrimental to the little people's well-being. However, I would be only too delighted to come and give them my renowned pep talk about pulling themselves up by their own shoelaces (if you allow them any). My secretary will furnish you with my standard list of fees on demand (please enclose s.a.e.).

Yours faithfully

Alexander Charles Prosser

TEST 377: MELANIE

Dear Sir or Madame,

A mungst my post this mourning was your litter offring to solicit poor and neeedy children for money those are luvly legs my deer. I'm shocked to the kwik if it's a bit too hot in heer let me help you off with that love. How dare you? It is well known that the bizzy execative has to unwind and the harder he striives to overcum his unforchewnate start the further he will go, here we go, here we go, here we go.

I have a natchurelly genrous spirit talking of spirit a sip of this will help relax you my pet. A monuterry contribushun would undoutedly be detrimental to the little peeple's well-being. Talking of well-being, wouldn't you be happyer lying down here. However, I would be only too delited to come and give them one and I know what I'd like to give you heh, heh know what I mean. My secretry will furnish you on demand and talking of demand put your hand here and feel this ouch put the pen down first you stupid girl.

Ooh

Mr Prosser

Who Got The Job?

If you have any executive potential, you will undoubtedly have picked both Melanie *and* Enid.

Melanie, I agree, is the obvious choice for a personal assistant and I've been well satisfied with her – regularly. True, her letter is not quite perfect but in these days of spell-checking word processors the odd minor spelling error is easily rectified – which is where Enid comes in handy.

Admittedly, Enid is dowdy and not the greatest of fun at the compulsory weekly office toga party, but my wife appeared highly delighted when I introduced her as my new secretary and no longer minds when I work late any more. And I know the office is in capable hands when Melanie and I are forced to attend all those boring but unfortunately far too frequent business trips abroad.

GET LOST MISS JONES – OR HOW TO GET RID OF YOUR SECRETARY WITHOUT HAVING TO PAY A FORTUNE IN REDUNDANCY MONEY

Like everything else, a secretary has a sell-by date. On no account should you keep a secretary longer than two years five months. Even

I'M AFRAID YOU'RE OVER-QUALIFIED, MISS JOHNSON — PARTICULARLY THE KARATE BLACK-BELT

the dimmest creature will eventually pick up things about your business which you would rather she didn't know.

It is vital that you safeguard your business secrets by maintaining a rapid turnover of secretarial talent. Besides, the attractions of even the prettiest of doxies become commonplace after a while. Just like cars, you should upgrade to a new model every now and then to keep you pinky and perky.

Unfortunately, thanks to the present idiotic labour laws of this country it is no longer easy to fire people willy-nilly, thus robbing executives of one of the chief pleasures of office. Cunning is therefore called for. If you aren't going to get stung for redundancy money you must force the employee to leave of their own accord.

While you'll miss her little ways – the massaging of the feet in the morning, the soothing of the brow and the inability after two years to remember how many sugars you like – you must be strong. Besides, it's so much fun, particularly if you win the sweepstake on how long it's going to take!

How To Transform Your Secretary Into A Goodbye Girl

- Get into the office before her every day and blunt her pencils
- Wire a new plug on to her electric typewriter
- Have her word processor flash subliminal messages at her
- Have the janitor flash rather less subliminal messages at her whenever she walks down the corridor
- Borrow her handkerchief every time you sneeze
- Water her pot plants with Domestos
- Drive her mad during dictation by repeating every sixth word three times, while drumming your fingers on the desk
- Swap the parting in your hair from the left to the right side
- Change to a diet consisting entirely of garlic, baked beans, hard-boiled eggs and apples

Always remember that an intelligent secretary is a dangerous secretary.

TRAGIC ~ EVER SINCE I TOLD HER SHE LOOKED BEAUTIFUL WITHOUT HER GLASSES, SHE REFUSED TO WEAR THEM

PHONEY EXCUSES

Where secretaries are concerned, protection is all important. They are the last line of defence between you and the steaming, grimy, grubby masses who want to sell to you, entreat you, beg for jobs, beg for jobs back, lick your boots or ask when you'll be home to dinner.

Life is too short. A tycoon's time is too precious. A good secretary would lie down in front of a speeding train rather than let through an unwelcome call. Unfortunately, this means one tends to get through secretaries at a fair lick.

I once had a superb secretary, Sherri, an incredibly talented lady, who managed to deflect even the most persistent of phone callers. Sadly, her own protection proved rather lacking and she had to leave me when she began to show. In return for my generously handing her a cheque for £50 to help her on her way, I insisted that she write down her favourite phone excuses, so that I could train future secretaries in the art of evasion.

Here's looking at you, Sherri. Best £50 I ever spent.

Sherri's Phoni Excuses To Protect The Boss

- 'I'm sorry. I was trying to patch him through on the car phone but I seem to have lost him in the Dartford Tunnel'
- 'Well, if it's really important, I *could* interrupt him. I'm sure Her Majesty won't mind'
- 'Can you keep holding? There are only another thirty-three verses of the company song to go'
- 'I'm sorry but his helicopter has to maintain radio silence until it clears Iraqi air space. I'm sure you understand'
- 'I'm afraid he's being interviewed by "The Money Programme" at the moment'
- 'I'm afraid he's being interviewed by the police at the moment'
- 'I'm afraid he's got a toffee in his mouth'

LEARNING HOW TO USE THE PHONE – OR WHAT THOSE TELEPHONIC PLATITUDES REALLY MEAN

In business, the telephone is the most important tool you can have in your hand. It's amazing how much fun you can have with it, particularly as so many people haven't the slightest idea how to make the most of their phone.

Some top businessmen are so masterful that they are able, with a flick of their finger, to make their staff jump through flaming hoops or balance beach balls on their noses (two performances daily).

Yet no matter how dominant they are in person, it's amazing how many become gibbering idiots over the telephone. Without being able to see the face of the person they want to browbeat, they become so lost and helpless that they commit one of the cardinal errors and begin telling the truth. Nothing, I need hardly tell you, absolutely nothing, is more dangerous where business is concerned.

Telephone-speak is like learning to speak a foreign language. But whereas all other foreign languages are a complete waste of time for an Englishman, this one is essential. Learn it well, and it will help you on your way to the top.

With my help, you too can gain mastery of your appliance.

You need never be afraid of your phone again!

Telephone-Speak – What You Say And What You Mean

'And what are you up to these days?'
'Keep talking and you might give me a clue as to who the hell you are.'

'I'm glad you rang. I've been trying to get hold of you all day.'
'Damn, I thought I'd told the switchboard to give you the bum's rush.'

'What a surprise to hear from you.'
'When did you get out?'

'We must have lunch soon.'
'1996 has a wonderful ring to it.'

'I'll get back to you.'
'Just look for the pigs flying past your window.'

WELL, FANCY YOU CALLING ME NOW — I WAS JUST THINKING ABOUT YOU!

'How are the wife and kids?'
'Particularly the wife.'

'Well, hello. I certainly never expected to hear from you.'
'As soon as I finish this call I'm sacking my secretary.'

'You went to that conference last weekend, didn't you?'
'I have in my hand some very *interesting photographs.'*

EXTRACTS FROM MY PRIVATE FILES

The Art Of The Memo

There's a lot of guff spouted about art. Some bozos get their kicks from gazing at paintings of dead people (even if they've got their clothes on), listening to old-fashioned music that sounds like a cat on heat, or paying through their noses to watch wallies prancing about with bananas down their tights.

But I know what I like. For me, nothing is more beautiful to behold than the well-crafted business memo.

The busy tycoon, omnipotent though he may be within Head Office, can't be everywhere at once. It's extraordinary how complacent, safe and secure those employees in the furthest-flung corners of your business empire can feel if you're not careful. Fun though personal surprise visits to these places may be, the most cost-effective means of exercising your control is the well-honed memorandum.

The perfect memo is like a sophisticated form of guerilla warfare. One minute, all's quiet on the Western Front. The next moment, devastation, death and destruction have been wrought, with nothing more than a few well-chosen words.

Here's one of my very favourite salvoes:

From: **Alexander Prosser**
To: **Harry Sherman, Managing Director, Do-You-Now Exhaust Centres**.

Harry,
I've just had a glowing letter from a satisfied customer, absolutely thrilled that one of our Stay-Fresh exhausts has lasted for three years and is still going strong.

Our friendship goes back to our first day at school. I've had faith in you all these years. And what's the result? – You ruin my business, you bastard.
You know as well as I do that those bloody things are supposed to fall to bits the second the one-year guarantee runs out. Turnover will plummet if this sort of thing carries on.
Fortunately, it won't. I've found a new supplier willing to comply with our standards of built-in obsolescence. And speaking of obsolescence, the new managing director arrives tomorrow.

Bye-eee!

You've exhausted my patience. Brackets, ha-ha, joke, close brackets. No don't write brackets down, my dear.

Prosser

PS Love to Doreen and the kids.

How to Maximize Those Profits

Too many tycoons, complacent with their own businesses, get bored and start searching for new ways to make profits. I'm as keen on a hostile takeover as the next man. But I've always been surprised how, with a little careful housekeeping, you can manage to squeeze still greater profits out of those companies already under your control.

It's a bit like rummaging around for coins down the back of an old settee (if you've got a hand free). No matter how well my managers tell me that they've looked, I can always find that little bit more hidden away in the fluff in some shady corner.

Always be on the lookout for new ways to maximize your profits. Here are a couple of letters from my files demonstrating my relentless pursuit of extra dosh.

Remember. Every farthing saved is a farthing made.

SAMPLE LETTER A

Sonny Patel,
Bottomley, Pratt and Patel, Shysters-at-Law
15, London Wall
LONDON EC2 17th June 1991

Dear Sonny,

Guess what I was doing in bed last night? Give the boy a cigar. Well, after that I was reading the Companies Act, looking for any loopholes you had overlooked.

Eureka! As you know, the present bunch of deadbeats and morons on my board are costing me a total of £578,563 a year. Do you realize that *nowhere* does the Act say that company directors have to be human?

Chessington Zoo is currently running an Adopt-An-Animal campaign. How much can it cost to adopt eight monkeys and put them in grey flannel suits, for goodness' sake? We should be able to get them for peanuts (geddit?). We'll also be the first firm in the country to issue its directors with company tricycles.

It should make for an interesting photograph in the Annual Report this year. What's more, I'll bet you a pony – no, better make it a monkey – that nobody notices.

See you at Henley. Bring some bananas.

Best wishes

Alexander Prosser.

SAMPLE LETTER B

Dr Jeremiah Bodkin Addams
Chairman
The Golden Oldies Corp.
c/o Bide-a-Wee Resting Home
Precipice Hill
nr. Bournemouth
HANTS

Dear Doc,

I've just received a scribbled, drool-soaked note from one of

the decrepit old bats in your care, complaining about the 'grossly appalling conditions' at the Bide-a-Wee Resting Home. There is a serious question that has to be answered here, namely: How the hell did my mother get my address?

Frankly, Doc, her letter has shocked me to the quick. I had no idea how out of hand things had become at the Bide-a-Wee. My mother complains at having to live on her own in a room measuring 10 foot by 12. Disgraceful!

Surely a frail old woman nearing the end of her days doesn't need that much space? You should be able to squeeze at least another two beds into the room. After all, the wrinklies are going to be lying down together soon enough. Isn't it a good idea to acclimatize them now for the next stage in life's journey?

Mother also complains of intense boredom, of being left on her own for hours on end with nothing to do. This is not on, Doc. Psychiatrists tell us that old crocks are happiest in their twilight days if they are doing something productive.

There is a government contract for stamping out number plates which was going to go to Wandsworth Prison that I reckon I can swing. I feel I owe it to my mother and her arthritic cronies to provide them with some healthy occupational therapy. After all, as my dear mother never tired of telling me when I was a boy, the Devil makes work for idle hands. Won't she be thrilled that I've remembered what she spent my childhood beating into me?

I hope that these lapses are not indicative of Golden Oldies Corp. as a whole. Our prospectus boasts that Golden Oldies Corp. exists to provide shelter, warmth and care for our silver-haired loved ones, so it is vital for our reputation that we maintain standards. It is also vital for our corporate plan that we lift profit margins of this sub-performing division of the Group this year from a lamentable 16% to a minimum of 45%.

I'll be down for my annual inspection in a month or so. I expect to see a marked improvement in conditions then.

Love and kisses to Mummy.

Yours sincerely

Alexander Prosser.

Dear Moneybags – The Agony Column For Worried Businessmen

I'll be the first to admit that it's tough at the top. For not only have you got to run your own business, but now that you're in this exalted position everyone else expects you to run their businesses for them as well.

I don't know about you, but unlike bloody John Harvey-Kipper-Tie, I'm not prepared to dish out free advice to all and sundry. If people want my opinion, they've got to show me how much they value it. That's why, when I agreed to do my famous *Dear Moneybags* column (now syndicated in 184 countries), I insisted that the correspondents expressed suitable gratitude for the inestimable advice they received.

For anyone who's been living in a cellar in Beirut for the past few years and might not have seen it, here's a little taster of my column, which is admired the world over.

Extract: June 1st, 1992.

GROMMETS GRUMBLER

Dear Moneybags,

I love your column but I never, in a million years, thought I would find myself writing to you.

I have 'a friend' who owns a small but thriving manufacturing business in the Midlands (you won't get your grommets cheaper anywhere), and I – I mean he – suspects that some low-down, conniving, rat of an asset-stripper is thinking of bidding for his company.

What can he do? He is 53 (albeit very youthful looking) and too old to have to work for a living. You are his last hope, Moneybags.

Yours,

Up A Gum Tree In Walsall.

Dear Up A Gum Tree in Walsall,

Call yourself a businessman? 'A friend' indeed. There's nothing to be ashamed of. This problem happens to many men at your time of life.

It's a piece of piss. Parcel up your latest profit forecasts or some other price-sensitive information and send it to him by registered post to record the fact that he receives it.

Now that the low-down, conniving rat of an asset-stripper is in possession of inside information, a bid for your tinpot operation will be illegal.

You owe me one.

Kindest regards,

Moneybags.

* * *

Extract: June 8th, 1992.

WHINGER FROM WALSALL

Dear Moneybags,

Help! The bastard who was after my business went away with his tail between his legs like you said he would. For the first time in ten years I felt relaxed enough to take a holiday!

But when I got back I found that some *other unprincipled bastard* had bought my company from out of the blue! I can't go on.

What did I do wrong?

Yours,

Even Further Up A Gum Tree In Walsall

Dear Gummo,

What did you do wrong? You wrote to *Dear Moneybags*! Terribly sorry, mate. Couldn't resist it. Those really are great grommets. Thanks for the tip-off. What a bargain!

Love and kisses,

Moneybags.

SO YOU STILL THINK YOU'LL MAKE A TYCOON?

Self-Assessment Test – Part Two

So you've now got a teensy-weensy bit of the company that's all your own to play with.

You can do a deal, use a phone, write a memo, rack up a few bob on expenses, bankrupt a small businessman or two and sack your staff with no compunction.

Who's a big boy then?

Well, *you're* not! There are probably hundreds of others within your own company in just the same position as you, just as tough as you, just as determined as you and just as smug, self-satisfied and stupid as you.

You think you're getting to the stage where others in the company will notice you? You're right.

Now is the *really* dangerous time for you. You've called attention to yourself and, by doing so, have revealed yourself to be a threat. A threat still puny enough to be easily eliminated. The blood's in the water. The sharks are all around you. It's kill or be killed.

Have you still got what it takes? It's time to evaluate yourself again – *honestly.*

Which Of These Applies To You?

(Make sure nobody's looking over your shoulder during the five minutes you are allotted to fill this in)

- I never waste a good idea, when one of my colleague's will do instead
- I make friends easily
- I lose embarrassing relations even more easily
- I support the Conservative Party
- I support the Monster Raving Loony Party
- I consider myself smarter than most of my bosses
- I am too smart to admit that I am smarter than my bosses

Part Two

DANGER – BASTARD AT WORK

3
Doing the Business

Are You Snake Enough to Climb the Ladder?

By now you should have a staff under you; a little house-broken menagerie all your own to play with, and if they're not calling you a bastard behind your back, you're doing something wrong. If any of them dare call you bastard to your face, then you know you're destined for greater things. You should applaud their spunk – and then fire them.

Sometimes saying 'you're sacked' just isn't enough. Once you've done it a few hundred times, there's no enjoyment left in it. You must learn to be more creative, more vindictive and more imaginative *pour encourager les autres.*

One way or another, you must learn to fire your staff with enthusiasm!

THE TEN MOST ENJOYABLE WAYS TO SACK YOUR EMPLOYEES

In the Caring Nineties, too many wimpish bosses delegate the sacking of employees to some faceless creep in personnel. Why should they have all the fun?

Those wimps refuse to admit that sacking people is one of the greatest perks a boss can have. A particularly vicious and public sacking will improve staff performance for days and does wonders for your morale. Don't be shy. Go ahead, make your day.

- Invite yourself to Sunday lunch at their house. Eat and drink all you

WE'VE BEEN A GREAT TEAM, JOHN BUT THERE'S ONE DIFFERENCE BETWEEN US. I'M FIRED WITH AMBITION — YOU'RE JUST FIRED!

can then, as you leave, remark that 'the garden is looking a bit run-down. But you'll have a lot more time for it, because . . .'

- Wait until 5.55 on a Friday evening in order to spoil their weekend. Score extra points for a Bank Holiday. Give yourself a gold star if it's Christmas Eve. Two if they have children
- When they wish you a Happy New Year, say sadly, 'Not for you, I'm afraid'
- Move their office into the toilet
- Move the toilet into their office
- Send them an invitation to a surprise farewell party. At the height of the frolics, have the kissogram girl announce that it's theirs
- Run a 'Spot the Sackee' competition in the house magazine
- Relocate the entire office while they're on a month's business trip to China
- Relocate the entire office while they're out to lunch
- Have the company plane sky-write 'Goodbye Jenkins' at the firm's annual sports day.

SNAKES AND LADDERS

You are an eager young executive whose talents are, as yet, unrecognized by the firm. Everyone at Head Office is invited to the Chairman's house for the annual staff drinks party. You spend the week beforehand in front of the mirror, practising holding a paper plate full of food and a drink in one hand while shaking hands and proffering your business card with the other.

The great day dawns at last. With some trepidation, you don your newest Marks & Spencer's suit and your best Hush Puppies and head for the heart of Hertfordshire, stopping at a motorway service station to buy their most expensive bunch of flowers for your hostess.

Arriving at the picturesque village of Huffleigh half an hour early you spend the time re-reading your car manual. You then motor up the meandering half-mile drive, marvelling at the splendour of the Chairman's seventeenth-century country estate which, according to *Country Life* magazine, is worth nearly £5 million. A feeling of ambition and aggression overpowers you and you vow to do everything possible

at this party to ensure that one day you too will be at the top of the corporate ladder.

Snaking your way through the BMWs, Porsches and Jaguars, you park your Lada and make your way to the house, handing the flowers to the butler when he answers the door.

As you make your way inside through the crowded throng, someone spills a drink down the front of your trousers. Doubled up to conceal the stain, you go looking for the lavatory. You open the wrong door and find yourself alone in the great man's study. You can't help but notice that on the desk is a confidential list of proposed staff cuts in your department. To your horror, you discover that your name is on it. Do you:

a) Sob, go back to the office and clear out your desk?
b) Plead, wheedle and throw yourself upon the Chairman's mercy?
c) Tippex out your name and replace it with that of your main rival?

You sneak outside for some air, hoping that nobody saw you, and then wander round the garden. While examining the roses for traces of greenfly, you spot your immediate superior canoodling in the shrubbery with the Chairman's wife. Do you:

a) Stammer, apologize and pretend you haven't seen anything?
b) Take your clothes off and join in?
c) Show them the polaroids, and let the lady start the bidding?

Your walk takes you past the garages and stables. As you stroke the Chairman's Bentley, you notice that the car has one dangerously bald tyre. Do you:

a) Take your jacket off, roll up your sleeves and replace it with the spare?
b) Find the chauffeur and order him to do it?
c) Loosen the nuts on the other three tyres and cut the brake cable?

Entering the house at the back, you find yourself in the kitchen. While you are replenishing your glass, a very drunk director reveals that the company will shortly be making a takeover bid for a rival firm. Do you:

a) Sober him up with some strong black coffee before lecturing him on the dangers of loose tongues?
b) Quickly buy shares in the target?
c) Quickly buy shares in the target before contacting the other company and offering to sell them the information?

On your way to the food, you are assailed by the boyfriend of an attractive secretary in your department who works for a competitor of your firm.

Pushing you behind a suit of armour in the hall, he whispers in your ear that in return for a better job and more money he will steal his employer's client list for you. You know that the list would be of immense value to your firm. Do you:

a) Tell him that your company would never dream of employing anybody so disloyal?
b) Offer him the job and pray he doesn't do the same to you?
c) Give him the job to get hold of the list; then sack him, claim the credit and bed his girlfriend?

Having stacked your plate too high with free food, you fail to see Zippy, the family poodle. You go flying headlong into a Ming vase which falls to the floor and smashes into smithereens. Do you:

a) Confess all to the Chairman and offer to pay for the damage out of your salary over the next forty years?
b) Find some superglue and try to glue it together?
c) Wrestle the Chairman to the ground and ask him if he often has such violent blackouts?

The Chairman's fifteen-year-old nympho daughter invites you into her bedroom to see her Pony Club rosettes. As she locks the door, you realize that she has an enormous crush on you. Do you:

a) Give her one of your jelly babies and then make a run for it?
b) Give her a lecture on the evils of under-age sex?
c) Give her a practical demonstration of the joys of under-age sex?

As you emerge from her bedroom, you are grabbed by the Chairman's forty-five-year-old sex-starved wife, who invites you into her boudoir to see her collection of erotic Indian woodcuts. As she slips into something unbelievably more comfortable, do you:

a) Throw your jelly babies over her shoulder to distract her and then make a run for it?
b) Let her throw you over her shoulder, while closing your eyes and thinking of the company pension?
c) Throw her over your shoulder and suggest a mother-and-daughter threesome?

When, later that evening, you manage to escape from the room, the Chairman's saucy seventy-five-year-old mother rolls up to you in her wheelchair and suggests a spot of how's-your-father. Do you:

a) Suggest a grandmother, mother and daughter foursome and then bring out the cards?
b) Give her a lecture on the evils of over-age sex?
c) Suggest a grandmother, mother and daughter foursome and then bring out the cards and cut for who goes on top?

In the midst of energetic congress, the like of which would have been excised from the Kama Sutra, the door to the bedroom flies open. The Chairman strides to the wardrobe and is on the point of picking out a fresh shirt when he suddenly notices, also in the wardrobe, you, his wife, his mother, his daughter and Zippy the poodle.

The Chairman's pacemaker short-circuits, his heart fails and he falls to the ground, writhing around on the floor in agony. Do you:

a) Rush to the Chairman's side, sobbing and begging his forgiveness?
b) Finish what you are doing, then go down to the garage to get a pair of jump-leads?
c) Do the decent thing for once in your life. Go back into the wardrobe to comfort the Chairman's wife, mother and daughter – and free Zippy the poodle.

How Did You Do?

If your answers were mostly:

(a) You are a cowardly, craven wimp of the first order who poses no threat. As such, you are ideal 'yes-man' material and I, for one, will be proud to have you on my board one day. Carry on toadying and you'll go far. But not too far.
(b) I am disappointed in you. Haven't you read anything in this book? You're an evil, back-stabbing, double-dealing bastard, without a grain of loyalty. In other words, you're too soft by half to get to the top. Shape up or ship out.
(c) Congratulations! You're on your way to the top. Now look out behind you.

HOW FULL IS MY WALLET – OR HOW TO MANAGE YOUR CASH FLOW

Managing cash flow is the vital ingredient of every profitable business. No matter which bit of that business you are now controlling, its success – and yours – depends upon how quickly you can suck in the money, and how slowly you let it dribble out.

One of the great joys of working for a large company is turning the screws on smaller companies. It's my second favourite boardroom sport. And, as in so many other things, size is everything. The bigger you are, the more pleasure you can have. There's nothing quite so exhilarating as watching a small businessman squirm as you explain why you haven't been able to pay him for the past six months before you tear up his tarmac with your company Porsche.

The government is fond of saying that the small businessman of today is the big businessman of tomorrow. It is your job to make sure that he becomes the bankrupt of tomorrow rather than the threat of tomorrow.

This handy little aide-memoire should be pinned up on the wall of your accounts department and woe betide any employee who pays any bill before 160 days is up. It's guaranteed to work – or your money back. (But just you try and get it, buster!)

Why The Hell Haven't We Had Our Money?

A) When they *are asking:*

- Because the cheque is in the post
- Because the cheque is in the Yugoslavian post
- Because only our finance director can sign cheques, but both his wrists are broken
- Because the mice got into the petty cash
- Because the accountant got into the petty cash
- What invoice?

Why The Hell Haven't We Had Our Money?

B) When we *are asking:*

- Because we need it for the Chairman's heart operation
- Because, within the business community, it is important to maintain face – as well as eyes, teeth, nose, limbs and kneecaps
- Because we'll tell our mummy on you if you don't
- So we will release your wife and children

THAT'S ENTERTAINMENT

Only those who know nothing about business think that it involves nothing more than getting together in a boardroom for half an hour's argy-bargy, at the end of which you shake hands, sign on the dotted line and walk away with the deal in your pocket. That might have been all fine and dandy in the days when you could buy Manhattan Island for a handful of glass beads (something which will soon be possible again, of course), but it's about as much use now as a woman on the board.

You'll soon learn that there are two ways of doing business in today's cut-throat, no-holds-barred, dog eat dog-shit world. You can set up a meeting, lay on sandwiches, drinks and crisps – and lose the deal. Or you can set up a meeting, lay on sandwiches, drinks, crisps and a bit of rumpy-pumpy – and win the deal.

Business entertaining is an art far more sophisticated than anything Michelangelo ever came up with. Fortunately, it is made considerably

SORRY – I STILL HAVE THE SAME CASH-FLOW PROBLEM I HAD WHEN YOU WERE MY COMPANY'S MAIN SUPPLIER

GONE BUST

PLEASE HELP

easier by the fact that you are invariably dealing with randy, greedy men who are some distance away from home.

In business entertainment, you can bet your arse that style and class are everything. Show the suckers a good time and they'll show you the colour of their money. Here, from experience, are the most sure-fire ways of entertaining businessmen.

How To Entertain – Before The Deal Is Done

- The Royal Box at the Royal Opera House, accompanied by the delightful ladies from the 'Sure 'n' E-Zee' Escort Agency
- The Members Enclosure at Royal Ascot, accompanied by the delightful ladies from the 'Sure 'n' E-Zee' Escort Agency
- Centre Court at Wimbledon accompanied by the delightful ladies from the 'Sure 'n' E-Zee' Escort Agency
- Dinner at the Savoy, accompanied by the delightful ladies from the 'Sure 'n' E-Zee' Escort Agency
- The British Grand Prix at Silverstone, accompanied by the delightful ladies from the 'Sure 'n' E-Zee' Escort Agency
- A night of bliss with the delightful ladies from the 'Sure 'n' E-Zee' Escort Agency, accompanied by the delightful ladies from the 'Slap and Tickle' Escort Bureau

[You may think that all this entertainment would soon become very expensive, but you surely know me well enough by now to guess who the controlling shareholder of the 'Sure 'n' E-Zee' Escort Agency and 'Slap and Tickle' Escort Bureau is.]

WARNING! We have got to face up to the harsh reality of modern life and realize that occasionally, very occasionally – hard though it is to believe – you will be doing business with some *woman*. I know, I know. I can only assume that some firms find it extraordinarily difficult to get staff. But fortunately these days the escort agencies are as broad-minded as I am, and I am told that Alphonso, Raoul, Tom, Dick or Harry go down a treat.

POST-DEAL ENTERTAINMENT

Once you've got the pigeons eating out of your hand, then you want them to fly home to their nests as quickly as possible, enabling you to get on with your next deal. Unfortunately, having experienced the ultimate in business entertainment, they may have developed a taste for it. In this case, one will have to wean them off it gently. But it is important not to offend. Here are a few creative suggestions for business entertaining once the ink has dried.

How To Entertain – After The Deal Is Done

- Breakfast at McDonald's
- A night out at an Andrew Lloyd-Webber musical
- An open-top sightseeing trip around London
- Dinner at McDonald's
- An all-day visit to the company plant in Slough

TOUGHENING UP EXERCISES – HOW MANY TIMES HAVE YOU BEEN A BASTARD AT WORK TODAY?

Even if you've got the right psychological profile to be a tycoon, it isn't enough on its own.

Are you tough enough to crack it before it cracks you?

Now is the time to separate the men from the boys – and the boys from the girls' blouses. You want to be the man with the big boots; you don't want to be the stuff he steps in.

Being a bastard doesn't come naturally to everyone. Unless you were born with a rhinoceros hide and a temperament to match, you must work at it. Even I didn't get to be me overnight. Once I was a mere 13-stone junior executive, the sort of runt who is always having sand kicked in his face. Now I have a team of men to kick sand in other people's faces for me.

Here are a few valuable exercises to help you develop suitably tough backbone, teeth and claws:

Stage One: Absolute Beginners

As a novice, you should be able to:

- Make a secretary cry (beginners should aim for twice a day and work their way up)
- Short-change the canteen lady
- Run over the car-park attendant's foot as you manoeuvre your way into your parking bay
- Reverse back over it to score double points
- Infuriate the security people by getting into the building by showing your bus pass instead of your identity card, each day for a week
- Steal a box of paperclips

Stage Two: Intermediate

If you have been doing your exercises diligently, you should – without flinching or undue strain – now be able to:

- Make a secretary cry six times (or two secretaries sob three times each)
- Park your car in the Chairman's bay
- Beat your head against a brick wall
- Beat your rival's head against a brick wall
- Remove all the toilet paper from the executive lavatories
- Rip a telephone girl in half
- Alter an appointment with your staff three times in a day – and then disappear off for a game of golf
- Do your famous imitation of the Chairman to his face
- Steal the coffee vending machine

Stage Three: Advanced

(WARNING: Before attempting these advanced exercises, you should undergo a complete medical check-up)
Now you're ready to really flex those muscles. Go for it! If you're true tycoon material, you should now easily be able to:

- Make a secretary cry thirteen times (or the entire typing pool simultaneously)

I'M SORRY YOU THINK I'M A ROTTEN BASTARD, MISS ARKWRIGHT — I WAS *TRYING* TO BE A REALLY *GOOD* ONE!

- Make a secretary
- Make the Chairman's secretary
- Make the Chairman's wife
- Make the Chairman's wife walk home afterwards
- Bankrupt a competitor
- Bankrupt a friend
- Steal the mainframe computer

4
A Businessman Abroad

Bugger La Différence

Assuming you have so far successfully stepped over the steaming cowpats which splatter the field of business, it shouldn't be long now before you're sent on your first business trip abroad. With my expert know-how, you should be able to sail through this like an old sea salt, unless of course you are still thrilled about a night away doing business in Wolverhampton – in which case there's a cowpat with your name on it heading straight for you.

Like so many other areas of business, the most important thing is that even if it is your very first time doing business with Johnny Foreigner, you must still give the impression that you have been doing it all your life.

For a start, if you want to appear a seasoned traveller your luggage should not be spanking new, but should look as if it has already been around the world twenty times. Although it isn't in their publicity handouts British Airways offer exactly this as a special free service to all their passengers. By the time your baggage eventually arrives, it will look older than you.

Once your baggage has been aged for you, you should never let it travel in the hold again. You're too busy to have to wait hours for it at your destination. Fortunately, airline rules on hand-baggage apply to everybody else, not to you. In the air, the businessman takes priority over women, children and other nonentities. Whatever the airlines say to the contrary, they really want you to take everything you need with you into the cabin as hand-baggage. The stewardesses will recognize you at once for what you are.

Many people are picky about where they sit, fussily expressing a

I'VE HAD ALL MY JABS BUT I DON'T BELIEVE IN TAKING CHANCES
AIR FRESH

preference for aisle or window seats. This is only a problem for junior executives. My advice is, as soon as you can, book both and then you don't have some wally from Wisconsin selling bathroom sealants sitting next to you. It also ensures you have room for your reading material, lap-top and stewardesses.

Films on planes tend to be terribly unimaginative, but not when I'm around. I have boosted the spirits of many a plane traveller by taking along my own films to liven up the monotony of air travel. While the bimbos are busy serving the food, I swap these with the existing cassettes. *Nancy Nurse Turns Out The Lights* and *Terror At 20,000 Feet* have always gone down a bomb.

Of course none of this applies to me any more as I've had my own private jet, the Mile High Club, for years.

The days when doing business abroad was an adventure are, I am glad to say, over. Hotels, of whatever class, are now the same the world over. You can get just as good a plate of fried sausage, eggs, bacon, mushroom, black pudding, tomato and chips in Bangkok or Bali as you can in Burnley; while, thanks to the wonders of modern technology, there's almost no hotel room in the world where you can't pick up *Birds of a Feather*, praise God.

Almost everything nowadays is standardized. Wherever you do business in the world things will be comfortingly familiar: food, drink, transport, skirt. The only thing that hasn't been standardized yet is the foreigners themselves.

You aren't going to progress very far in the business world just shafting Brits. You're going to have to learn to stick it to foreigners as well. This is one learning experience that should be great fun . . .

HOW TO DEAL WITH THE EUROPEANS AND OTHER BLOODY FOREIGNERS

Oh, for the halcyon days of Empire, when dealing with the natives was all black and white. Things were a lot easier when the map was splattered with pink. These days we've got all nationalities under the sun to contend with and the coves get frightfully touchy if you can't remember which bally country they come from.

It's all right for the overpaid, time-serving politicians who have done

very nicely thank you out of Europe, what with all those gratis overseas junkets and plenty of duty-free and tottie on each trip. While they've been stuffing their faces with frogs' legs and knackwürst, look at the mess they've lumbered us with. Our money's being thrown away on wine lakes we can't sup, butter mountains we can't spread and foreigners we can't stand. We fought two World Wars (at least those of us who couldn't swing reserved occupations) only to see the sods now buggering about with our currency, our agriculture, our sausages, our women and our pints.

But enough about diplomacy. Europe isn't going to go away, I'm sorry to say, and so we have to learn to deal with it. I've been doing it for years and what I don't know about making foreigners jump through burning hoops isn't worth knowing.

It is important when dealing with our European colleagues to understand that they are obsessed with what they laughingly call history. I don't mean *real* history like Pig-Sticking in the Raj. No, they're always wittering on about the grand, historic tradition of Europe, about how it's the birthplace of civilization, the cradle of democracy, the home of the arts and things like that. All that means is that some guy invented an aqueduct and another painted a ceiling. So what?

All you need to know is that we Brits have fought and beaten hollow *every* European country except Portugal – which has been our ally for five hundred years – and Luxembourg, which we couldn't find. So much for history. We can't just think of them as all simply being foreigners any more. These are more enlightened times and if you aren't going to be shown the door (la porte, das Door) you have to be able to distinguish what sort of foreign they are, even if they do all look the same. Here is all you need to know about successfully doing business in Europe.

The French (Frogs)

We can learn a lot from the French. They have many sterling qualities, including an ability to produce and sell cardboard apples; a taste for barbecued British sheep; a deep and lasting gratitude for our rescuing them repeatedly in two World Wars; an admirable economy with soap; and an amusing fondness for pharmaceutical suppositories.

The important thing to remember about doing business with the

French is that they lie, they cheat and you can't believe one word they say. This means we ought to get on well with them except that they do all their lying in French which no British businessman worth his salt can speak. The way to communicate with the French is to speak English . . . very loudly . . . until they understand.

The problem with the French is that they have never forgiven us for beating Napoleon. My opposition to the Channel Tunnel (nothing to do with my operating a ferry company) disappeared when I discovered that this end of the cross-channel link terminates at Waterloo. That should remind them who's who.

The Germans (Krauts)

People try to stereotype the Germans. They claim that they are a cheerless, militaristic, aggressive, ill-mannered, bombastic, punctilious and regimented race. They are absolutely spot on.

I can't think of the number of business meetings with Germans that I have tried to enliven with my famous impersonation of Hitler about to commit suicide in the bunker. It never fails to go down a treat at the firm's annual dinner dance, but not once have I got a laugh from any of the hundreds of humourless Huns I've done business with over the years.

Still, what can you expect from a country that eats itself into a stupor with pigs' trotters, cabbage and dumplings so leaden they could have been dropped on Coventry? My advice is to stuff yourself before you go to Germany and not eat again until you clear German airspace.

Let's not beat about the bush here. They are a race of fat, drunken, slobs. Yet I *still* don't like having to do business with them. However, it has to be said that they do have an awful lot of money . . .

Note: All this also applies to the Austrians but we don't have to be so polite about them as they're not in the European Community.

The Italians (Eyeties)

There's nothing I can tell you about the Italians that you haven't already learned by trying to order a pizza or a contract killing in this country. Like the deaf, they only understand wild hand gestures and distorted facial expressions.

They are happy, smiling, agreeable, easy-going and family-minded folk and doing business with them is a breezo. Take as many disposable female personal assistants as there are contacts to meet. You won't see your PAs again until you leave the country, but all the contracts will be signed.

The Dutch (The Dutch)

Caps, dykes, bicycles – the Dutch are sex mad. So could somebody please explain why they are so boring?

Drugs and prostitution are legalized. Which is why it's a bad place to do business, but a great place to take your holidays if you've no time to get to Thailand.

The Spanish (Dagos)

Tall, blue-eyed, blonde and with a great love for winter sports and beating each other with birch twigs, these people are never happier than when locked in a small pine room, throwing water over hot coals and sweating their socks off.

It is a well-known fact that it is physically impossible for outsiders even to say 'hello' in their language without dislocating their tongues. It is thus pointless trying to do business with them.

Or am I thinking of the Swedes?

The Danish (Pastries)

See 'The Spanish'.

The Belgians (Flems and Walloons)

Boring people. Great chocolate.

The Irish (The Oirish)

To us British, the most foreign of all European nations. Shamrocks, leprechauns, shallalies, shamrocks – the Irish are a thrusting industrial

BERLI
BERLIN
CLICK

nation. Just a few more years at their current pace and they'll be in the exact same position as Britain . . . in 1856.

The Greeks (Zorbas)

Olive trees, olive oil, olive skin.

They say you should beware of Greeks bearing gifts. I'll second that. In twenty years of doing business with them the only thing I was given free took my man in Harley Street two months to cure.

The Luxembourgers (De Luxes)

I can't speak highly enough of this wonderfully clean, beautiful and efficient country. Nowhere else in the world can you meet such warm-hearted, generous, intelligent people.

It's the ideal home for my nearest and dearest. So much so that several of my companies and the odd bank account are now domiciled there.

The Portuguese

Thanks to our long-standing friendship, the Portuguese are unique among the European nations in liking, admiring and trusting we British. So, in doing business, it's a doddle to walk all over them.

The East Europeans (Slobbering Slavs)

Russians, Serbians, Poles, Litvaks, Lithuanians, Turks, Estonians, Georgians, Albanians, Croatians, Slovenians, Ruritanians, Bulgarians, Hungarians, Mongolians and Czechs.

I have only one word to say about doing business with Eastern Europe: *don't!*

Namby-pamby politicians who couldn't negotiate their way out of a carrier bag never tire of telling us of the business opportunities that are opening up in Eastern Europe. This is true, providing you are happy to be paid in wet fish, flared jeans, extremely soft fruit, reject mobile missile launchers and those incestuous wooden dolls fitting snugly inside each other.

The Americans (Yankee Doodles)

If you hear your first name being yelled across a room and see, bearing down upon you, an outstretched arm and a gleaming set of teeth, then you know you're about to do business with an American.

Americans are friendly, open, generous and gregarious. All the more reason to distrust them. You've only to look at their smug behaviour in WWI and WWII (the even more popular sequel) to get a true insight into their national character; in both instances dragging their feet until completely convinced we were about to win, before charging over the hill like the 7th Cavalry and claiming the victory as theirs. No prizes for guessing who collared the merchandising rights.

Still, what can you expect from such a mongrel melting pot, a nation that combines all the charm of the Krauts, the intelligence of the Irish, the integrity of the Italians and the dress sense of the Scots? Their only redeeming feature is that they inherited their good looks from the English.

The Japanese (Yella Fellas)

The Japanese are a cruel, sadistic people who have never forgiven us for Alec Guinness. Of all the trading partners you'll encounter, you'll find them the most remote and inscrutable. The Japanese don't like foreigners, which is laughable considering how foreign they are themselves. I'm the last person to think in terms of stereotypes, but the Japs really are tiny, all look alike, have no sense of humour, are a nation of brown-nosing workaholics and are totally obsessed with miniaturization – which is bad news for Japanese women.

HOW TO SPEAK FOREIGN

Occasionally, just occasionally, you may come across some foreigner whose English is so pathetic that he doesn't understand you. On these rare occasions – for most of them are well-trained these days – it is worth having some useful words and phrases up your sleeve. I have found that these few well-chosen ones will cover pretty well any eventuality.

WELCOME TO THE U.K., MR SHERMAN— I DO HOPE YOUR TAILOR MAKES A FULL RECOVERY

TEXAS-LONDON

Swedish

1. Pundhuvud!
2. Far åt helvete!
3. Din fru är frigid. Tro mig, jag vet.
4. Hela min boloagsstyrelse sänder sina hälsningar till din läckra dotter.
5. Jag har just övertagit ditt företag. Här än en plastpåse så du kan tömma ditt skrivbord.
6. Ditt ansikte påminner om en babian-ända.
7. Är alla i ditt land lika dumma som du?
8. Skall du ha en snyting, pappskalle?
9. Du kan ta ditt kontrakt och stoppa upp det i häcken, amigo.
10. Det har varit ett nöje att göra affärer med dig.

German

1. Schwachkopf!
2. Verschwinde!
3. Deine Frau ist frigid glaube mir, ich weiss es.
4. Mein gesamter Vorstand gruesst Ihre heisse hungrige Tochter.
5. Ich habe gerade Ihre Gesellschaft uebernommen. Hier ist eine Plastiktuete fuer die Ausraümung Ihres Schreibtisches.
6. Sie haben ein Gesicht wie das Hintern eines Pavians.
7. Ist jeder in Ihrem Land so dumm wie Sie?
8. Wie wuerde Ihnen meine Faust auf Ihrem Auge gefallen?
9. Mit dem Vertrag koennen sie sich den Hintern abputzen, mein Freund.
10. Es hat mich gefreut, mit Ihnen Geschaefte zu taetigen.

French

1. Crétin!
2. Va-t'en.
3. Vôtre femme est frigide. Je vous assure je le sait.
4. Mon conseil de directeurs entière envoie leur sentiments distingués à votre fille delicieuse.

5. Je viens d'acheter vôtre société. Voici un balai pour nettoyer vôtre bureau.
6. Vous avez un visage comme la derièrre d'un singe.
7. Est-ce-que tous vos compatriotes sont stupides que vous?
8. Je vais te coller mon poign dans ta gueule, espèce de crapule.
9. Vous pouvez prendre ce contrat là, et le bourrer dans ton cul, amigo.
10. C'était un plaisir de traiter avec vous.

English

1. Cretin!
2. Piss Off!
3. Your wife is frigid. Believe me, I know.
4. My entire board of directors send their regards to your luscious daughter.
5. I've just taken over your company. Here's a plastic bag/brush to clear out your desk/office.
6. You have a face like a monkey's bottom.
7. Is everyone in your country as stupid as you?
8. How would you like a knuckle sandwich, mush?
9. You can take that contract and stuff it up your jacksie, amigo.
10. It's been a pleasure doing business with you.

Part Three

STAYING ON TOP

5
What *About* the Workers?

The Staff Are Revolting

Are you becoming impatient? Don't feel powerful enough yet? Not getting enough adrenaline buzz?

What you need is a visit to the shop floor. You know, I know and your colleagues know that you're just one jumped-up little tick half-way up (or half-way down) the ladder. Executive you may be: tycoon you're still not.

But handle a plant visit shrewdly and, to the proles on the shop floor, you're suddenly the heavy honcho from Head Office. Play it right and they won't have the slightest idea what you're doing there (much like you). From the lowest fitter to the highest plant manager, they won't know whether you're there to de-unionize, modernize, open or close them.

Shove on a white coat, slam on a hard hat, pick up a clipboard and stride around the plant making notes and looking purposeful. They'll cringe from you, cower from you and hide from you. They'll be terrified of you. You'll have a *wonderful* time and feel on a heavenly high for months.

You have tasted power. Make it to the top and you can taste it for every minute of every day.

(*Warning!* You should be aware that pointless plant visits are a favourite sport among executives at every level. Take considerable care that one of your superiors has not had exactly the same idea as you on the same day. This could spoil your lovely day out – as well as your best pair of trousers.)

... AND WHAT EXACTLY ARE THOSE FUNNY LITTLE THINGS OVER THERE BY THAT CONVEYOR-BELT?
THE WORKERS

A PLANT VISIT

You're finally 'management'. Just one step below board level. Big deal! The higher you climb, the harder you fall and to anyone other than a moron it's blatantly obvious that you're being set up for the biggie. You were pleased as punch when the Chairman picked you personally to go to the Peterborough rubber products plant to plug a sudden plunge in profitability.

It is only as you are packing your briefcase that someone, laughing their socks off, points out to you that you are the fourth executive despatched on the same task – and none of the others have been seen since. You realize you have been sent on a kamikaze mission.

You pick up the phone, undecided whether to ring a headhunter or your mother when you're struck by the notion that this could be a test of your mettle. After all, isn't there a place on the main board coming up soon? You cut the phone line by biting through the cord and head off courageously for your appointment with destiny.

You set off for Peterborough. You realize that first impressions are everything but also know that there has been considerable industrial unrest in the plant in the recent past. Do you:

1) Stun them with your importance by arriving in the company helicopter and landing on the roof?
2) Irritate them by sweeping up in your chauffeur-driven Jaguar and parking in the shop steward's bay?
3) Placate them by driving your Jag yourself – to an adjacent street, where you switch to a waiting clapped-out Mini that the company keeps for just such purposes?

With a squeal of brakes and the smell of burning rubber, you alight from your vehicle at the run. A worried-looking management deputation races out to meet you. For the first few minutes, you ignore them completely as you wander round the exterior of the plant, noting the peeling paintwork, the cracked and broken windows and the plants growing in the guttering. Do you:

1) Chastise them for letting the company's assets go to seed and order that the plant be redecorated forthwith?

2) Applaud them for not wasting the company's money on inessentials?
3) Point out that the plants appear to be marijuana and order the setting up of a new private division with the profits split 80/20?

With the management still in tow, you continue your investigations with the thoroughness of a bloodhound. Rooting around behind a stack of pallets at the rear of the plant, you come across a grassy area where the ground is strewn with used contraceptives. The managers hide their heads in embarrassment as you tell them that you are shocked to the core. Do you:

1) Berate them for permitting such lax morals in the plant and insist that the grassy spot be concreted over?
2) Order the contraceptives to be washed and repackaged?
3) Admonish them for allowing the staff to use the company's product without paying and suggest that the women involved be sent to you individually in the manager's office to be punished?

Two hours later, after a punishing session with the miscreants, you are now ready to inspect the plant. Demanding to know why productivity at the factory is so piss-poor, the management tell you that the plant is monstrously over-staffed and that there's no one left who will accept voluntary redundancies. You smile that smile you've been perfecting for months and tell them to 'just leave it to me.' Do you:

1) March to the personnel department and order them to issue compulsory redundancy notices to 30 per cent of the workforce?
2) March to the personnel department and order them to issue compulsory redundancy notices to anyone with an 'R' in their name?
3) Don a gas-mask, radiation badge and protective clothing and roam the factory with a geiger counter, shaking your head and muttering all the while: 'Such a tragic waste of human life!'

Now that the workforce has been trimmed to a manageable size, you turn your attention to the product itself. You discover that the plant has been manufacturing condoms in three sizes, 'small', 'medium' and 'large'. There are unsold stocks of the 'small' size stretching to the

ceiling. You turn on the managers, calling them all the names under the sun for their monumental stupidity and for failing to see the solution under their noses. Do you:

1) Order that the small ones be relabelled and exported to Japan?
2) Order that the small ones be distributed free to schoolchildren – after being relabelled 'water bombs'?
3) Order that all of them be relabelled, with the three new sizes 'large', 'extra-large' and 'gigantic'?

By the end of the month, demand for the product has increased five-fold. However, instead of being pleased, the Chairman is furious with you and is after your blood. You discover that he had been planning to run the plant into the ground so that it could be closed and the land redeveloped. Because of your brainstorm, the Chairman's pet project has gone up in smoke. Your entire future is in the balance. Does the blaze at the factory start with:

1) Your matches?
2) Your cigarette lighter?
3) The Chairman's cigarette lighter?

The factory is razed to the ground. You are raised to the board. The Chairman is arrested for arson and insurance fraud.

Congratulations on a job well done!

How did you do?

1–6: You obviously only need the small size packets.

7–14: Medium for you, my boy. Keep your hand in and it'll come to you given time.

15–18: Gigantic. At last, a man nearing my own stature!

HANDY PHRASES FOR THE HOI POLLOI (WHEN YOU CAN'T AVOID THEM)

It's extremely important for any company Chairman to recognize the importance of, and show respect for, everyone who toils within his company – even the grubbiest little oik on the shop floor. From time to time, you'll find it necessary to visit some of your plants (remember

to order some plastic sheeting to be put down on the floor first) and it is amazing how much good you can do for management relations just being seen getting down on all fours and chatting to the common workers on their level. And what a wonderful photo opportunity it presents.

Although the workers are often overwhelmed when someone as great as you stops to accept a Woodbine and a chat, you can almost feel the warm glow you leave behind you while you climb back into your chopper and wave a fond farewell as they clutch onto their caps in the wind. If you've never had to do it before, here are a few opening conversational gambits that I've never known fail to put the worker chappies at their ease:

- 'I envy you your job, mate. I'm sure it's more honest and rewarding than being Chairman and Chief Executive.'
- 'That's an amusing calendar. There's a girl in the Renoir on my office wall a little like that.'
- 'Don't worry about missing work by chatting to me. You can stay late to make up for it.'
- 'Gosh. Spam! Do they still make it? I'm sure it's much better for you than the massive filet mignon we've just ploughed through upstairs.'
- 'You've no idea just how much we at the top appreciate all you little people at the bottom.'
- 'You'd be paying a fortune at a health farm to get the sort of exercise you're getting here.'
- '50 miles per gallon? You're a lucky chap. My Rolls only gives me 12.'
- 'Oh, good. Smoking like that, I don't suppose you'll worry too much about the asbestos problem here.'
- 'I SAID HOW CAN YOU WORK WITH THIS BLOODY NOISE GOING ON?'

WAYS TO IRRITATE YOUR STAFF,

Or The Pick Of Getting Up Their Noses

Whoever said that being Chairman was dull? Some lesser executives have no better way of relieving the monotony of their working day than playing with an array of stupid office toys on their desk.

I MAY BE YOUR CHAIRMAN
BUT I'M NOT AFRAID OF
GETTING MY HANDS DIRTY.
TO PROVE IT...

...PUT IT THERE!

But when you become Chairman, you have a far greater source of considerable amusement just outside your door – your staff, and you are only limited by your imagination.

Although one should not show it to the plebs, being Chairman is immense fun – and the more staff you have, the more fun you can have. Any Chairman worth his salt can have endless hours of jollity and pleasure at his staff's expense, pulling their strings so they jerk around like demented puppets – and there's not a blessed thing they can do about it if they want to keep their jobs.

So get out there and start getting under their skin. After all, what's the point of having scaled great heights to become the boss if you can't be bossy – annoying your staff to pieces just as your bosses annoyed the hell out of you when you were a lowly minion?

You are in a position of power now. Use it. Enjoy it. Revel in it. Flaunt it, baby, flaunt it!

Here Are A Few Of My Favourite Ploys. Try Them. You'll Like Them:

- Fart loudly in their office and revel in them trying to pretend they haven't heard – or smelt – anything
- Whistle while you work
- Exercise your *droit de seigneur*
- Whistle while you exercise your *droit de seigneur*
- Call a meeting for 5.55 P.M. on a Friday
- Call a meeting for 5.55 P.M. on a Friday – and ring up from the yacht at 8.30 to say you can't make it
- Always get their names slightly wrong
- When one of them does a good piece of work, always praise someone else
- Leave a document talking about the need for rationalization in the photocopier
- Play golf like a drain and watch them desperately trying to play even worse

JOHNSON? — JOHNSON? — AH! **JOHNSON!** — YOUR WIFE'S THE ONE WITH THE CUTE BIRTH-MARK ON HER BOTTOM

6
All Aboard!

Dealing with Directors and Shareholders

Hip, hip, hooray! You're now on the board of your company. The workmen are digging up your garden to put in your swimming pool, you lunch every day at the Institute of Directors and your waistline grows three inches in the first month. Best of all, you are at last able to take advantage of that greatest of corporate inventions, the service contract. Once you have signed this magical piece of paper you've got it made, whatever happens.

Even if you turn out to be a more incompetent director than Skippy the Kangaroo would have been and are kicked out on your jacksie tomorrow, the firm will have to pay you what you would have earned over the next three to five years in one glorious lump. If you fall out with your fellow directors, you'll still get your lump. If the company gets taken over, you'll all get your lumps. Everybody wins – except the shareholders!

Remember how much fun you used to have as a sprog playing leapfrog? Well, now you can have that fun all over again, except that this time it's so much more rewarding because it's played with real money.

The joy is that although you will now be paid an obscene salary, you can truthfully claim that it is forced upon you by others, against your will. It's all the fault of the remuneration committee, comprised of non-executive directors – those part-time chappies who don't actually do anything in the company and only turn up for board meetings. You're not to blame if they happen to be directors of other companies and, as a result, are keen to see you paid as much as possible so that they can ask for similarly ludicrous salaries.

True, you're also a non-executive director of other companies and have the power to restrain such greed. But it would be terribly rude of you when you're working with them just two or three days a month for a minor king's ransom not to reciprocate by way of thanks.

All this cash, all this responsibility and all this power should make you happy as a sandboy. But it doesn't. Because there's still some stupid old fart with hair growing out of his nose called the Chairman running *your company*! It's a situation that must not be allowed to continue for much longer. And it won't . . .

MEETING THE GREAT UNWASHED – OR HOW TO FOOL ALL OF THE SHAREHOLDERS ALL OF THE TIME

If you think you have problems with moronic idiots within the company, wait until you have to start dealing with the shareholders. If they're still looking for the missing link, why don't they go along to an Annual General Meeting some time?

Some shareholders can be really uppity, acting as if they own the company. Which, unfortunately, they do. No matter how much you may inspire fear and loathing within your own company, when it comes to the AGM, it is a whole different ballgame – and it is your balls that they are after. But that's no reason to let the little bastards walk all over you. Some directors can cut the mustard at the AGM and others wimp out. Yet for every one who stands transfixed in the lights like a frightened rabbit as the shareholders mow him down, there is another able to milk the audience like a herd of contented dairy cows.

In my time, I have faced every sort of question from meddling investors who think they can run the business better than I, and have refined every possible answer. When facing shareholders, you must remember that more important than anything else is honesty. Once you can fake that, you've got it made. Over the years, I have found that just ten simple answers will cover every possible contingency posed by the punters. It appears to make no difference in which order you use them.

New balls, anyone?

DIRECTOR
UNDERLINGS' ENTRANCE

PROSSER'S 10 HANDY ALL-PURPOSE AGM ANSWERS

- I'm so glad you spotted that. We were sure somebody would.
- Grossly overpaid? No, I certainly wouldn't say that.
- Nepotism? In this company? Nonsense! My son is the most highly qualified of all my children for the post.
- I sold those shares for purely personal reasons. I'm not a mind-reader. How was I to know the company would announce the biggest loss in its history?
- You're looking well this year, my dear. How old did you say you were? No, of course I'm not trying to get out of answering an awkward question. Next please.
- I *know* we all had chocolate digestives last year, but in this period of belt-tightening we could only afford them for the directors this year.
- No, I don't know what happened to that nice little white-haired man sitting next to you last year.
- That question is really for the finance director. Unfortunately we haven't been able to reach him since he left for a week's holiday in the Cayman Islands . . . six months ago.
- I'm so glad to see that they let you out for the day again. The AGM just wouldn't be the same without you.
- Golly, is that the time? We don't want to keep you busy people a moment longer than necessary. I think I hear the free bar opening at the back.

THE DIRECTORS' JOKE BOOK

Now that you're a director, you're going to be wagging chins and hob-nobbing with fellow directors all over the place, at the CBI Conference, the Institute of Directors, Wimbledon, Henley, Ascot, Madame Henrietta's or wherever.

What on earth are you going to talk about? You've devoted so much of your life to work that you've never had much time for socializing. Too late, you discover it's now a vital part of your job.

Don't despair. You'll learn straight away that such conversations are almost invariably about the parasites that feed off companies,

as directors get their own back at the lawyers, merchant bankers, stockbrokers, PR people and the other scum who make our lives a misery – and then charge a fortune for it.

To avoid making any gaffes or dropping any vital information when in your directorial cups, you should never talk about your work or your company. Instead, have the assembled mob eating out of your hand, with selections from my Directors' Joke Book, full of guaranteed, sure-fire jokes, witticisms, sallies, bon mots, jests, quips and japes.

Practise in front of your staff, complete with appropriate hand gestures, docking them a day's pay if they don't laugh. You'll be amazed how quickly they are roaring with uncontrollable laughter and how quickly you gain the necessary confidence.

I Say, I Say, I Say!

Q: How many lawyers/merchant bankers/stockbrokers/PR people* does it take to screw in a lightbulb? [**Delete as appropriate.*]
A: How many can you afford?

Q: Why don't sharks bite lawyers/merchant bankers/stockbrokers/PR people?
A: Professional courtesy.

Q: What's brown and black and looks good on a lawyer/merchant banker/stockbroker/PR person?
A: A Rottweiler.

Q: How can you tell if a lawyer/merchant banker/stockbroker/PR person is lying?
A: His lips are moving.

Q: What do you call 10,000 lawyers/merchant bankers/stockbrokers/PR people chained together at the bottom of the sea?
A: A good start.

Q: How do you get a lawyer/merchant banker/stockbroker/PR person down from a tree?
A: Cut the rope.

. . . AT WHICH POINT, THE VICAR'S DAUGHTER TOOK OFF HER WOODEN LEG AND SAID, "WHY DIDN'T YOU **TELL** ME THE GOLDFISH WAS DYSLEXIC?!"

LAUGH OR YOU'RE FIRED

Q: What do you give the lawyer/merchant banker/stockbroker/PR person who has everything?
A: Five years.

Q: What do you have if you have five lawyers/merchant bankers/stockbrokers/PR people buried up to their necks in sand?
A: Not enough sand.

Q: What do you call a former lawyer/merchant banker/stockbroker/PR person?
A: Waiter!

Thank you, ladies and gentlemen, and good night!

7
Life at the Top

The Final Frontier

THE GOSPEL ACCORDING TO SAINT PROSSER

And the Lord said, for 364 days of the year, thine is the blessed company and with it thou can do exactly what thou jolly well liketh and I willst not punish thee, honest.

Yea, thou canst pay thyself a salary of biblical proportion, thou can create two sets of books, thou canst fornicate with thy secretary and with thy directors' wives while coveting all their asses, thou canst hire and thou canst fire and thou canst generally rob everybody rotten. For, saith the Lord, that is the role of the Chairman.

But, on the 365th day, the Lord saith thou shalt wear the hairiest of shirts and be dragged screaming to the AGM and a plague shalt be upon thou and thou shalt suffer suffering the like of which is known only to company chairmen and the plague shalt be called the plague of shareholders.

And verily the shareholders shalt be old and doddery and insipid of hearing and they shalt demand of thou the answer to questions of such monumental stupidity that thou wouldst rather gnaw thy own leg off than endure a second longer. And verily the plague shalt want feeding and the feeding of the five thousand shalt have nothing on the feeding of a horde of effing shareholders, all of whom willst smite each other for the biscuits with the chocolate onst top.

THANK YOU, LORD,
FOR EVERYTHING YOU'VE
DONE FOR ME — FROM
NOW ON I'LL ONLY
BE COMMUNICATING
BY FAX

And the Chairman shalt be sorely tried and shalt make an exodus from the AGM in a winged chariot, swearing to throttle the next miserable sinner of a shareholder who dare crosseth his path, proclaiming that vengeance shalt be his and vowing to take the company private forthwith.

But in the midst of his trouble and woes, the Chairman shalt be comforted by the thought of his enormeth thalary, by Ruth, Naomi and Sarah, his veritable tribe of hand-maidens, and by his humble abode in the land of Belgravia, his humble abode in the land of Oxon and his less than humble abode in the Isles of the Caymanites.

And throughout his travails and sorrows, he shalt also remember that he is not alone. The Lord is with him. The Lord sees everything. And the Lord loves a good laugh.

HAVE YOU MADE IT TO THE TOP? – THE FINAL FRONTIER

You are relaxing on a lilo in the swimming pool of your 300-foot yacht, *Business*, (amazing how often you're away 'on Business'), having coconut butter massaged into your lithe, lissome body by one of your personal assistants while another is reading sexily to you from a dossier prepared on a possible takeover target.

As your yacht is preparing to dock in Antibes Marina, the Captain rings from the bridge to tell you that the 305-foot yacht of your deadliest rival, *The Lady-What-Lady-That-Was-My-Wife*, is occupying your berth.

You jump up, scattering personal assistants and papers. As you throw on a few clothes, you notice that the naked mountain of blubber that is your hated rival is standing by the low railing of his yacht, gazing in your direction and sticking out his forked tongue. Do you:

1) Stick out your tongue in return?
2) Order your entire crew to stick out their tongues in return?
3) Order your entire crew to drop their trousers and moon in return?

Wobbling perilously close to the edge of the dangerously low railing, your rival is by now screaming invective at you in his native tongue and appears to be turning purple. Unless he cools off quickly, you fear that he could be heading for a heart attack. As your boat approaches his, do you:

1) Tell the Captain to turn the boat around and head back to sea?
2) Hold out a key so that you scratch the paintwork on your rival's yacht as you come in to dock?
3) Tell the Captain to ram your rival's yacht?

As your boat slams into his, you are mortified to see that your rival loses his balance and trips over the criminally inadequate railing, plunging headfirst into the Med, with the wash rocking your boat alarmingly as he goes bob-bob-bobbing along. His topless mistress bounces to the edge of the boat, screaming that he is drowning and begging you to do something. Do you:

1) Immediately throw off all your clothes – and ask him what it's worth to jump in and save him?
2) Immediately throw off all your clothes – and go sunbathing on the top deck?
3) Immediately throw off all your clothes – and nip across to his yacht to comfort his topless mistress?

Tragically, when you have finished comforting her – for the third time – you are too late to save him. Your rival is no more, floating belly up like a dead whale. Your marine lawyer advises that you cannot harpoon him and claim salvage rights. Do you:

1) Warn the coastguard that there's a danger to shipping?
2) Insist that a Spanish pathologist carry out the inquest?
3) Ring your stockbroker immediately with an order to sell as many shares in your rival's company as he can?

When the news of the sad loss to the business community finally reaches London, the shares fall savagely on the Stock Exchange as investors, fearing what will happen to the company now that there is no longer a strong hand on the tiller, dump their shares. Do you:

1) Rub your hands – and your dead rival's mistress – with glee as you contemplate your quick killing?
2) Order your on-board tailor to make you up a pair of black inflatable arm-bands?
3) Ring your stockbroker immediately with an order to *buy* as many shares in your rival's company as he can at the lower price?

You know it would be a cheap, despicable and disgusting act to take advantage of your rival's demise. You recall the unwritten code of honour amongst tycoons. You also recall that there's nothing in writing. So do you:

1) Make a takeover bid for his yacht?
2) Make a takeover bid for his mistress?
3) Make a takeover bid for his company?
4) All three?

Your rival's company, yacht and mistress are all yours – and it still isn't midday. As you toast your good fortune with the excellent champagne in your new boat's wine cellar, you realize that you have two yachts on your hands. Do you:

1) Put a blue plaque on your old yacht and try to sell it?
2) Give the old yacht to your Captain as a tip?
3) Give the old yacht to your new mistress and go sailing off together on your His 'n' Her yachts into the sunset . . . ?

Are you now a tycoon, a true captain of industry or just another wannabe? With quivering hands, add up this all-important score

1-11: Start reading the book again from page 1 and this time concentrate, you pathetic bozo. You can read, can't you?

12-21: Tycoon? Don't make me laugh. Practice saying 'yes'. You're going to be needing it a lot for the rest of your career.

22: Congratulations! You have successfully completed my course. You are now a tycoon, free to enjoy all the perks,

I'D ESPECIALLY LIKE TO THANK MY DARLING WIFE, MY BROTHER, MY CHILDREN AND, OF COURSE, THE OTHER MEMBER OF THE PANEL OF JUDGES
BUSINESSMAN OF THE YEAR
BUSINESS AWARDS

privileges and pleasures that it entails. Just one little thing. Steer clear of Antibes Marina if you know what's good for you.

THE CHAIRMAN OF THE BOARD GAME

(© Alexander Charles Prosser)

Of course you can't play silly games with your directors. They are, after all, serious, strait-laced and self-important people. But here's a silly game you *can* play with them.

Your directors will pretend they want to discuss all manner of boring guff about the company, just as you did when you were brown-nosing your way to the top. But what's the point of this? You're not interested in their opinions, only in how loudly they say 'yes' to yours.

But that's not to say that board meetings can't be bags of fun. I like to get the boring, routine business out of the way as quickly as I can and move smartly on to 'Any Other Business', at which point I whip out my pride and joy: my *Chairman of the Board Game* (© Alexander Charles Prosser). Loosen up! You're Chairman! Have fun!

Rules of the Chairman of the Board Game

(© Alexander Charles Prosser)

1. Playing is compulsory.
2. Chairman has two moves for every one move by ordinary directors.
3. It's always the Chairman's turn when he says it is.
4. The Chairman can use his own dice.
5. The Chairman is always the racing car.
6. It's the Chairman's board and he'll get very, very cross and take it away unless you all play his way.
7. Game costs £1,000 deposit per counter (non returnable). Bumper jackpot prize is £50,000 (covered by Extraordinary Items in Annual Report).
8. The Chairman always wins.
9. The other players then stand and sing, 'For He's a Jolly Good Fellow' – thrice.

10. The Chairman shall of course be entitled to make up his own rules as he goes along and which can be enforced retrospectively.

The Board Of The Chairman Of The Board Game

Below are some of the squares on my Chairman of the Board Game, on which you can base your own version of the game. Get someone in your design department to knock you up your own set (mine is a de-luxe, gilt-edged, leather-tooled and jewel-encrusted board).

1. The *Sunday Times* names you Businessman of the Year. Go back three spaces.
2. One of your plants releases a dangerous amount of effluent into the Mersey. Nobody notices. Advance two spaces.
3. It's your birthday. Collect £500 from each player.
4. The *News of the World* uncovers your love nest. Stay in bed. Miss a turn. Turn a Miss.
5. Your second set of books are stolen. Hit player to your left.
6. Profits collapse. So does a player of your choice.
7. The company pension fund goes missing. The youngest player goes and stands on the window ledge.
8. The Fraud Squad arrives. Go back three spaces.
9. The Fraud Squad accept your bribe. Advance four spaces.
10. Your wife decides to take a sudden holiday. Sack the missing director.
11. You are caught in *flagrante delicto* with your secretary. Game stops for three minutes.
12. The Fraud Squad come back. Plant evidence on the player to your right.
13. You go to jail. Shuffle back a space.
14. It's Ford Open Prison. You start a new business empire there. Leap forward five spaces.
15. You take up tango lessons. Go back one space, forward three spaces, back one space, spin round and bow.
16. The board vote against you. Throw the other counters out of the window.
17. The board vote to depose you. The game is over. You have won. Sack the other players.

AM I
ENTIRELY
SURROUNDED
BY YES
MEN ?!

YES
YES
YES
YES
YES
YES
YES
YES

GOOD ~
JUST
CHECKING!

CHAIRMAN

PROSSER'S TEN BUSINESS COMMANDMENTS

I am always being asked by people – usually dismal no-hopers – how I have been so successful when those around me have so frequently fallen by the wayside, hit by illness, misfortune or the Fraud Squad. In former times, I would simply have told them to Piss Off. But now that my position at the pinnacle of British business is unassailable, I see no reason any longer to conceal the secret of my success.

Throughout my glorious business career, I have always kept certain inspirational tenets to the fore. Over the years, I have refined and honed these into ten basic business commandments; ten commandments which I follow religiously and from which I derive great comfort and guidance. Lest I forget them, I have a copy, inscribed in gold leaf upon vellum, hung on the wall of my smallest room (itself bigger than most of your rooms). Thus they are always with me at my most private moments.

They have been the guiding light of my life. Let them light up your life too and they shall lead you to the promised land, at the tippy-top of the business heap.

PROSSER'S TEN BUSINESS COMMANDMENTS

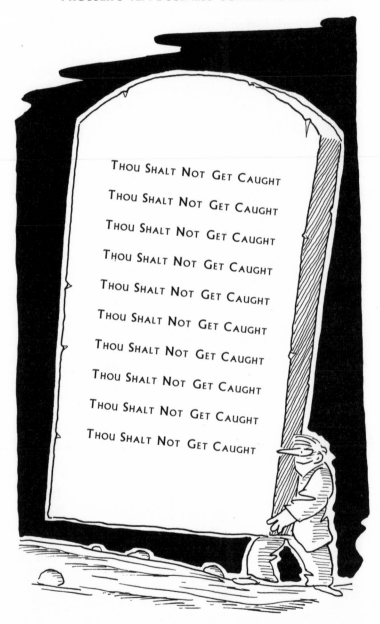

THOU SHALT NOT GET CAUGHT

THOU SHALT NOT GET CAUGHT

THOU SHALT NOT GET CAUGHT

THOU SHALT NOT GET CAUGHT

THOU SHALT NOT GET CAUGHT

THOU SHALT NOT GET CAUGHT

THOU SHALT NOT GET CAUGHT

THOU SHALT NOT GET CAUGHT

THOU SHALT NOT GET CAUGHT

THOU SHALT NOT GET CAUGHT